This book is dedicated to My Lord and
Savior Jesus Christ from whom
all blessings flow.

OTHER BOOKS BY MONIQUE R. RANSOM

Who Is Thy Neighbor?
Can A Christian Be Possessed By An Evil Spirit?

Unless otherwise indicated all Scripture quotations in this book are from the Authorized (The New King James) Version Copyright ©1994 by Thomas Nelson, Inc. Scriptures taken from the Holy Bible New International Version Copyright ©1993, 1978, and 1984 by International; Bible Society. Use by permission of Zondervan Publishing House. All rights reserved. Holy Bible, New Living Translation, Copyright © 1996. Used by permission of Tyndale House Publishers, Inc. Wheaton, Illinois 60189. All rights reserved, Definitions are quoted from Webster's new World Dictionary, Copy right ©1989, 1983, and 1979 by Simon and Schufter, Inc. Published by Western New World dictionary; A division of Simon and Schufter, Inc. 1 Gulf + Weston Plaza New York 10023. The Holman Bible Dictionary, Published by Broadman & Holman, 1991. All Rights Reserved. Used by permission of Broadman & Holman. Scripture quotations marked HCSB are taken from the Holman Christian Standard Bible®, Copyright © 1999, 2000, 2002, 2003, 2009 by Holman Bible Publishers. Used by permission. Holman Christian Standard Bible®, Holman CSB®, and HCSB® are federally registered trademarks of Holman Bible Publishers; Merriam-Webster's Collegiate Dictionary, Eleventh Edition copyright © 2008 by Merriam-Webster, Incorporated; Merriam-Webster Online Dictionary copyright © 2013 by Merriam-Webster, Incorporated.

Library of Congress-in-Publication Data:
Monique R. Ransom
ISBN-13: 978-0615780108)

Copyright ©2013 Monique R. Ransom, a.k.a Monique Marshall, a.k.a Monique Marshall –Johnson. All Rights Reserved.
Edited By: Dawn Wrenn
Retyped By Brittany A. Duplessis
Published By Create Space Publishing

No parts of this book may be reproduced in whole or in part, or transmitted in any form without written permission from the author, except by a reviewer who may quote brief passages in a review; nor may any part of this book be reproduced, stored in a mechanical, photocopying, recording or other without written permission from the author or publication company. For information email Monique R. Ransom at shespeaks3@aol.com

Declaring God's Glory

A FATHER'S LOVE

An Inspiring Book of Prophetic Poetry That will Encourage, Uplift, and Quicken Your soul!

By
Monique R. Ransom
Prophetess

In Loving Memory

Of

Bruce C. Ransom, Senior
(*Grandfather*)

Went Home: May 1998

And

Michael Brockington (Ransom)
(*Brother*)

Went Home: July 1999

And

Carolyn D. Lewis (Ransom)
(*Sister*)

Went Home: June 4, 2008

And

Trenton J. Marshall, Jr.
(*Son*)

Went Home: September 11, 2009

Declaring God's Glory

A FATHER'S LOVE

An Inspiring Book of Prophetic Poetry That will Encourage, Uplift, and Quicken Your soul!

By
Monique R. Ransom
Prophetess

Table of Contents

My Prayer..*13*

Acknowledgements..*16*

Introduction..*18*

The Father
Faith..*23*
Encouragement..*30*
Love...*36*
Wisdom..*43*
Encouragement..*52*

The Son
Sorrow..*61*
Love...*67*
Encouragement..*73*
Salvation..*82*

The Spirit
Mind..*90*
Wisdom..*100*
Encouragement..*107*
Love...*114*
Salvation..*122*

About the Author..*131*

Our Mission 133

Salvation *134*

Other Books *135*

Contact Us..*138*

From the rising of the sun and the going down of the same: I shall declare His glory among the heathens and His marvelous works among the nations.

Psalms 113:8
1st Chronicle 16:24

My Prayer

Lord, I enter into Your presence to ask for Your grace and mercy that is new to me every morning. I enter Your court with praise and thanksgiving not for who I am, but for who You are in me and all the You have done in my life.

I lie before Your feet humbly, but come boldly before You asking that you bless all that will read this book. I pray that the wisdom that You share with me they receive also. The love You show me in my hour of need, You show them too. That You allow them to prosper as their souls flourish and that You keep them in your perfect peace while giving them strength through joy.

God, only You know the needs of each. I ask that with your infinite wisdom, You meet each need. I ask that Your perfect will be performed in their lives. Until Your return, help them live their lives the way You intended from the very beginning, VICTORIOUSLY IN CHRIST!

This is my prayer Amen.

Acknowledgements

In my journey, and at the time this was written, I knew that I was not alone. Through God, many have been sent to encourage my soul and make this book of Christ's love possible. To my beautifully blessed children; *Renee, late son, Trenton Jr., Tyrone, and Sierra,* thank you for your patience, help and inspiration during the writing of this book.

Special thanks to all those who have inspired me to believe in myself and in the gift that God has given me: *Lisa*, where ever you are, you are truly an angel from above; *Janice McBryde & Wesley McBryde*, your encouragement and faith in God over me are truly priceless and cannot be measured by silver or gold, my love I give you always; *Marlo Chase & Monica Coatson*, for believing in me when the odds were stacked against me; my adopted mother *Reverend Mary Robinson*, the mother I never had, you support and encouragement mean the world to me. God's blessings are truly upon you because your presence in my life has been nothing but that, a blessing. To all who have believed in me in spite of myself; may God richly bless the lives of each and every one of you?

To all that have helped in the production of this book: my editor, *Dawn Wrenn* for her expertise as an editor and for her faith in me as a friend; and the printing company. To my *Pastors Bennett and Jean Donnell* of the *River of Life Christian Center*. You have been there for me in ways you could never imagine. The word of God you brought forth has blessed my life. Without the wisdom God so richly blessed each of you with, I could not have had the faith to believe that God had chosen me for such a task. Thank you and God bless you!

    A special Thank-You goes out to *Brittany Duplessis* for retyping this first and my second book. These new editions would not be possible without you. Thanks for letting me bend your ear as well as presiding over my cased. You were a fair judge!

    Finally, to all those who have been blessed by this book, I thank you for support

Introduction

In our journey through life there will be many challenges to face, many decisions to make and moments when we will embrace the unknown.

Circumstances will bring about changes to our plans. Dreams will sometimes shatter. Hope will be destroyed and our faith will sometimes fail us. It is in these moments with the unknown that we will wonder if we are standing alone. God, our Father wants us to know that He loves us dearly. He knows when we need just a speck of hope; a glimmer of light to shine its way with solutions to what ails us.

The Bible tells us that *"we are sheep to be slaughtered and many are the afflictions of the righteous"* (Psalms 34:19), but God delivers us from them all. This is something that is very important for us to know and hold on to. Many times we feel that God is selective or sometimes shows favoritism because we measure our lives against the lives of others, but God is no respecter of persons. We are all the same in his eyes. What He does for one He will do for another. He may not come the same way, but know that He is coming just the same. His timing is different for everyone and this is the part that is the hardest for us. The wait time! God takes your faith to the very end. We will reap if we faint not.

It is in that wait time we either feel like giving up or simply retreat with a defeated attitude thinking that God has forgotten us. He hasn't. He has heard every prayer. He has cried with you when your heart was troubled and He was there to rejoice with you when the victory came. You must understand that we are purged, formed and shaped during those moments. We are being prepared for an even greater battle that we are not yet aware of.

Although the pain and suffering we feel is real, it is not our attitude toward them that determines whether or not we find peace in our circumstances and situations. God already knows that we are more than a conqueror. We must know that too! Knowing who we are makes all the difference in how we complete the tests that God has placed before us or the challenges often created by the choices we make.

Being a Christian does not eliminate us from affliction, heartache and pain. As long as we live in this life we will have them, but what makes us different as Christians form the world is how we manage our trials and tribulations. When we realize that with God on our side, nothing is impossible, we can be victoriously is not always easy and will come over time, but we must determine our mind and heart as well as set our attitude toward being victorious.

Our trials and tribulations are God's good times. *"And not only so, but we glory in tribulation also; knowing that tribulation worketh patience; And patience, experience, and experience hope; And hope maketh not ashamed because the love God is shed abroad in our hearts by the Holy Ghost which is given unto us"* (Roman 5:3-5). It is during these times that God's love for us shines through. He pours from His spirit comfort in our darkest hours, joy in our sadness and peace to surpass all our understanding. God doesn't want us to go through life defeated, brokenhearted and down trodden. He wants us to live life victoriously. *"Nay... in all those we are more than conquerors through him that loved us"* (Romans 8:37). God wants us to know that He cares for us. That no matter what the problem, there is nothing too small or too great that he cannot fix or solve. God is unlimited with His mercy and grace towards us. He promises to us are for now and evermore.

It is my hope that this book filled with inspiring and prophetic poems of faith, hope, and charity will encourage your soul. This book was written to inform the mind and to bring hope while making changes in your life. Each poem was written from my heart and spirit, during my own personal trials and tribulations. I have opened up my heart and want to share my experiences with you while ministering to you about the realness of God in all our lives.

As you journey through your Christian walk, know that you are not alone. Many have made this walk before you and many will follow behind you until that glorious day when our Lord and Savior returns for us.

Until then, be blessed in the Lord and in the power if His might for He cares for you! My prayers are with you always.

Nay, in all these we are more than conquerors through him who loved us.
Romans 8:37 KJV

THE FATHER

And without faith it is impossible to please God, because anyone who comes to Him must believe that He exists and that He rewards those who earnestly seek him.

Hebrews 11:6 (KJV)

VICTORY

Love is the motivator
to faith.

Faith is the
activator to His spirit.

His spirit translates
the knowledge of God.

Together they equal
VICTORY!

God's Faithfulness

God is forever faithful
God is forever true
God has continuously blessed each
and every one of you

God is always gentle
God is always kind
God is the only one that realizes
the potential you have inside

God has already blessed us
with his continued faithfulness
So if God doesn't do another thing for us
we will still be blessed

Because He is

Faithful

God has already blessed
and is always faithful to us
He could have stopped at filling
our needs but said give
them what they want

He could have stopped at our
wants but gave us even more

His love is so faithful that He
even gives us the desires
of our heart

He is Faithful

With God Nothing Shall Be Impossible

There are times in our lives when we need the impossible to happen
Challenges arise and only a miracle will solve them
God is a miracle worker and is able to bring us out
By removing the temptations, the fears and all the doubts

We need to have faith in those areas that we are not at rest
It is our complete faith in Him that will bring out our success
We need to have faith in those areas that we are not secure
Only faith in God will bring about a solution or a care

Faith without action is like mankind without air
It suffocates the process until it is dead
Dead faith is like no faith at all
It leaves all your problems and situations unresolved

Faith is the only way to open up Heaven's airwaves

Without it you send your answers to die in an early grave
With God nothing is impossible as long as you believe
Faith holds the answers to complete victory

There's No Problem God Can Not Solve

When the storms in life are raging and
your world seems unstable
Know that God is willing and able
to see you through

That no matter what the problem
or how we think that He should solve them
God's love will guide us through it all the way

"Cause He's God and God alone
He sits up high but looks down low
There is no problem that's too small or too great

So, just be patient and you will see
How God will triumph and bring victory
to all who love him and are willing to obey

'Cause He's God and God alone He sits up high but looks down low
There is no problem that's too small or too great

And not only so, but we glory in tribulations also; knowing that tribulation worketh patience; and patience, experience; an experience, hope: and hope maketh not ashamed; because the love of God is shed abroad in our hearts by the Holy Ghost which is given unto us.

Roman 5:3-5 KJV

Count It All Joy

Count it all joy

> When you face those darkest hours and it seems all is lost and hope is gone

Count it all joy

> When the shadows of the footprints you see are yours and yours alone

Count it all joy

> When the pain seems too much too bare and you turn to see no one there

Count it all joy

> When the darkness that surrounds you becomes so overwhelming that you cannot see

Count it all joy

> Because through it all victory waits for thee

Count On Me

Count on me
> in the midnight hours when
> you are awake and all alone

Count on me
> in the morning when it seems
> all hope is gone

Count on me
> to be by your side no matter how
> tough things might seem

Count on me
> because I am your God
> and I care for thee

So Be Encouraged

In your search to fulfill one of God's promises to you

Know that He is standing there to see you through

It does not matter how many doors you have to unlock

Just keep pressing on and don't dare stop

Know that God will bring what He promises to them

Who so diligently seek after Him

SO BE ENCOURAGED

Staying Encouraged

In life things are sometimes tough
Trials and tribulations can get awful rough
but keep this one thing in mind and that is
these tests last just a short while
'Cause, Christ our Lord has been through it
all so there is no way that you can fall

Stay encouraged no matter how things
might seem
'Cause Jesus Christ will soon set you free
When it is over and you look back to
reflect on all that you have been through

Remember that there is another sister or
brother who needs just a little
encouragement form you

Hope In A World of Hopelessness

When things in life get sometimes rough
and it seems like the world is awful tough
there is only one in whom you can put
your trust and His name is JESUS

Our dreams and desires are often
shattered
It seems like nothing else matters
Everyone seems to have gone astray
but I know one who can make a way
and His name is JESUS

When all is lost and hope is gone
Don't give up keep holding on
Reach out to Him as He reaches out to you
and in His loving arms JESUS will bring
you through

He is Hope for a Hopeless World!

"Because he loves me" says the Lord, "I will rescue him; I will protect him, for he acknowledges my name. He will call upon Me and I will answer him; I will be with him in trouble, I will deliver him and honor him. With long life will I satisfy him and show him my salvation."

Psalm 91: 14-16

On God's Wings of Love

On God's wings of love
is where you will find me
Sheltered by His love,
I trust Him to guide me

They lead me to places
 I have never seen before
Places where dreams
and hopes live once more

They protect me through
life's storms and waves
And makes each of them
easier to brave

Because His wings surround me
both day and night
It is on God's wings of love
you will find my life

There Is No Loneliness In Christ

There are moments in our Christian walk
when we may feel we are all alone
We feel we have been abandoned and that
all hope is gone

In a twinkle of an eye, God our Savior will
provide the comfort and peace that we
need
To help us stand up against those
lonesome moments for just a little
company

God knows the need man faces to embrace
life with his own companion
But so many of us are impatient and go
through relationships taking many
chances

We must hold on to the fact that
God knows when the time is right
He will send you that special someone
who is guaranteed to stay for life

Be patient and do not hurry
to fill that void with just anyone
because God has already chose
them before the world begun

Loneliness

Searching in a world of darkness
to find just a speck of light
Oh God, just someone to hold
someone to show all the love
I have stored up inside

Wonder if I will ever find
the one who was chosen
for me since the world began
Or will I continue to face the rest
Of this life alone yet here I stand

So many wrong choices
So many dreams shattered
My heart torn on every side
Pounding and throbbing to release
all the love that strongly abides

Faithfully, I continue to hold fast
to promises of Him who I so dearly trust
To one day fulfill this life of mine
with someone I can love

As I continue to wait, not all the time
patient but waiting nevertheless
Waiting still for Christ to deliver me
from the awesome loneliness

God Is Not Far Away

God is not far away
God promises to be with us
every step of the way
No matter the problem
No matter the cost
God's love for us will exceed it all

He was there when were born
He will be there when we are old
His love for us has no magic
mystery or secret to unfold

It is in God we live and in God we die
In God we should put all our trust
For only He is able to keep
us all righteous and just

God is not far away
From our joys, sorrows triumphs or pains
God still remains faithful, loyal, righteous
and true
God is not far away because He cares for
you

Matters Of The Heart

When it comes to matters of the heart
One might get confused as to where it should start
The heart can provide many wonderful things
Joy and laughter are a few that it brings

Love is the one that stands out the most
because of the warmth from its gentle host
A love so special and one of a kind
Can sometimes be very hard to find
However, there is one special love that comes to mind

It is a love that is unconditional and true
Guaranteed to last your whole life through
It is not judgmental, harsh nor cruel
Neither does it contain envy or strife as a tool

It is gentle, kind and full of compassion
and does not change with every wind or every fashion
This is a love that only comes from our Lord above
Descending from heaven on the wings of a dove

He offers this love to any and everyone
It began on the day that He sacrificed His son
When it comes to the matters of the heart
Remember, that God's unconditional love is the best place to start

The thief cometh not, but for to steal, and to kill, and to destroy: I am come that they might have life and that they might have it more abundantly.

John 10:10 KJV

DECEPTION

Satan is the author of all confusion
He plays on the mind until he deceives you
Most if the time we think that our
thoughts are ours
but in actuality they are sometimes his
that he uses to devour

He will tell you this and he will tell you
that
He will tell you anything to get you off
track
He'll say that's a lie and that's not true
Constantly stealing the truth from you

He will paint all sorts of pictures in your
mind
'Til you find yourself going crazy inside
He will deceive you with promises of some
good things too
Don't Be Fooled! They are not guaranteed
to last for you

He has all sorts of lovely schemes
to keep you in bondage in his scene
He'll bring you closer and closer to him
until you are totally wrapped up in sin
He wants you soul at any price

There is nothing that he won't do or sacrifice

Our adversary will talk a very good game
While he slowly connives his way into your brain
He'll offer you anything to get you to follow him
Then once you are there, he will do you in

He knows how much time he is given
To bring as many souls into his prison
Where there is continuous gnashing of teeth and pain
Constant afflictions over and over again

There is only one way out
It is not east, north, west or south
It's through Jesus Christ, King of Kings
Peace, joy and love is what brings

How do you find Him I heard you say
By confessing on your knees as you begin to pray
Ask Him for forgiveness for all of your sins
Release all your burdens upon him

Now you are renewed and born again
and His spirit now lives deep within

Journey Down A Country Road

I woke early one morning to the rising of
the sun
Decided to take a stroll before the crowing
rooster begun
Along the walk I came across a man on the
side of the road
He asked if I had a moment just to sit with
him and talk

This man looked rather tired and his
clothes were dirty and torn
I wanted to keep on going, but instead I
listened as we walked
He began to tell about this man who is
kind in every way
He had stopped him on this same road to
talk to him one day

He said that when he met this man his life
was lost and in disarray
This man did not seem at all surprised at
the words that he had to say
You see everything had bothered him and
the world's stress became his own
Until the day he met this man on his
journey down a country road
This man looked a lot like him except his
heart was pure and clean

There wasn't a single word that was spoken that did not encourage me

The lessons that were taught were golden rules for us to live by
He said, "Man is appointed a day to be born and a day that he will die
Be not weary of heavy laden for I will give you rest
For as long as you live in this life you will have many tests
Be careful that you show my love have faith and always pray
Be thankful for everything that is good
And remember to share along the way."

Wisdom In Life's Lesson

As we travel through life
there will be many lessons to learn
It is from these lessons that our lives
will begin to turn and turn

Lessons produce knowledge that
is passed down from those who are old
Lessons passed from generation to
generation
all that has been sowed

In our lessons there is wisdom
that we often take for granted
We forget about the power
that stands strongly behind it

Wisdom comes from knowledge
that we suffer from lack of
They are mighty words given
from our Lord who sits up above

Without this knowledge
we are people doomed to perish
Nation by nation and all that we cherish
Let the wisdom in life's lessons
from God pass its torch from old to young
That it can continue to be expanded upon
and passed on to the next little one

How Long Is The Night?

Weeping may endure for a night
but joy comes in the morning
Psalms 30:5

But how long is the night
Ask Daniel as he lies in the lion's den
He will tell you that it seemed
like his night would never end

How long is the night
Ask Jonah as he toured around
through the belly of a whale
that had given him such a fright as they sailed

How long is the night
No one can really say
It depends on each circumstance
that may come our way

The question to be asked
in each testimony told
Is how long was your night
Before joy returned with its sweet delight

PROCLAMATION

Many Christians ride the fences all day
Compromising our Lord Jesus Christ' ways
Jesus is raising an army that will stand up
and proclaim that He is on his way back to
reign

It is time to yield ourselves to His
complete control
so that he can raise up strong and bold
Satan may think that he has the upper
hand but contrary to popular opinion it is
all in the Lords plan

He is cleaning out the churches and
reviving the land
Knocking down stronghold with the wave
of his hand
Either you are for Him or you are against
Him there is no in between
so come out from behind the screen
and claim Him as you King

Let your light shine! Hide it not under a
bushel because you will not count and
He will never be able to use you to the
fullest

How I hope and how I pray that your boldness
In the Lord grows each and everyday
so that together we can stand in the gap and give love
to those who have lost their way!

Proclaim!

Why are you downcast, O my soul? Why so Disturbed within me? Put you hope in God.

Psalm 42:5 KJV

The Walk of A Christian

The walk of a Christian is sometimes hard
The things we must change can become a strain but
Through it all you can rest assure that you are not alone
In both the good times and your long sufferings
God is with you

He shares in your joy and offers comfort in the pain
His live last through the sunshine and the rain
Rejoice in the Lord because He has chosen you to carry His message through

We must stand strong and in the power of His might because Satan plans to put up a fight
The load will get real heavy sometimes but do not be blind

After you have been through God has a blessing waiting at the end of the rainbow for you

An Uphill Climb

Life comes with many disappointments
No matter how things might seem at the time
There is a light at the end of that tunnel
a light that shines brighter than any sunshine

You must take a deep breath and begin again
Let faith become your closest friend
Focus your eyes on the one who holds
eternity in the palm of His hand
For this strength my friend
you will need to stand

With God nothing shall be impossible
to those that choose to believe
Cast all your cares upon him and He will sustain thee
So dry your eyes and wipe those tears away
Cause it is through God's love for us
that these things will change

He will reach out His unchanging
hands to comfort and uphold you
In His loving arms He will let you
know that things will be all right
He will then whisper softly in your ear,

"Don't give up the fight!"

He will be by your side through it all
So stand shake and brush those
unwanted spirits off because life's
disappointments are all a natural
part of the course!

Hold On!

Hold on just a little while longer
The trouble you face will soon be over
For the joy of the Lord is your strength
Fasting and praying will build your defense

This will help you keep peace of mind for you will find that
Jesus Christ, our Lord, has brought you through all that the enemy has laid upon you

Because He Cares For Me!

As I walk along the beach watching the beauty of the sun I reflect upon the moments we share and the day our relationship begun

The softness in your voice and the gentleness of your touch sends a warm feeling through my soul
I feel that I can relax and yield completely to your control

Knowing that you are always there whether it's morning, noon or night gives me confidence that I am never alone when God is by my side

Only you know my innermost thoughts my fears, my wants and needs
It's your consistent encouragement that let's me know I have nothing or anyone to fear

With You by my side I can safely abide in the strength of those loving arms
I know without a shadow of a doubt that You have kept me from danger and harm
Because He cares for me!

Struggles

O Lord,

As I sit here behind this wooden desk I look around at this great big mess
Thoughts are flipping and tossing throughout my mind
Some of every kind

Trying to hold fast to the dreams of tomorrow yet I sit here today in so much sorrow
I look at my life and wonder sometimes if I will ever find love and happiness in this lifetime

I know that there are many more tests and trials to face so I keep pressing on in this race
You have always shown me love, kindness and patience too
I hope that I will never fail you

If it were not for you I would have no life
Roaming around in a world full of strife
There is now a peace that lies deep within my soul trying to come forth strong and bold

If I could just keep this flesh of mine in check
Through the eyes of you Lord I would pass these tests

THE SON

Thou hast turns for me my mourning into dancing: Thou hast put off my sackcloth, and guided me with gladness; to the end that my glory may sing praise to thee, and not be silent. O Lord my God, I will give thanks unto thee forever

Psalms 30: 11, 12

Through It All!

In your times of sorrow and grief
God will be by your side
He will comfort you through those
difficult moments by providing you with
rays of sunshine

Although your grief of sorrow seems
like it will never go away
It is God's undying love for you
that is guaranteed to stay

There is no pain that He cannot feel
no tear He cannot see
There are no moments when God
is not near to provide you with
comfort and peace

Be encouraged and know
that you are not alone
That where ever faith and hope abide
God's love is there also

Through it all His presence is always near
To comfort and uphold those who love
Him and are so dear

Speak To My Heart

Speak to my heart
Dear Lord Jesus Speak to my heart for I
know that this is where I will find You
when my sorrows begin to start

Speak to my heart,
Lord Jesus when I ache
from sorrow and pain
Speak to my heart Lord Jesus so that I can
be free to smile once again

Your words are like a musical melody that
sings softly among my heart and soul
It leads me to that secret place where so
many mysteries begin to unfold

There you encourage me to keep fighting
and to keep holding on
To the dreams and the visions you gave me
before the storms of life dang its song

All of a sudden those things that once
tore my wonderful heart apart seem so
insignificant once You began to speak to
my heart

Where Is Your Victory?

The sorrows of death left its stench on the door of your heart
Someone you hold dear has gone and it tears your heart apart

Don't mourn for them but those who are still among the living
It is they who must continue
To live in this life full of many prisons

Don't mourn for them because they have found that perfect peace
Their souls are not at rest from life's battles with its enemies
Man has no say as to the time of its departure
Man can only pray that their souls will be free from an eternal torture

Death! Where is your sting?
The grave has no victory because
Jesus won and took the keys of death on the cross at Calvary!

Sorrows

With Christ
there are no sorrows
because Jesus
provides the hope
for your today's and
your tomorrows

Brushing My Sorrows Away

If you live long enough you will have
many days with feelings of sorrow
Days when peace no longer abides
and hope seems lost for tomorrow

Sorrow a feeling that comes when
we lose our faith and confidence in Him
I am who stands by your side closer than
any friend

Sorrow comes when we are disappointed
by situations that do not turn out the
way we thought that it should
Usually it is because the messages
we interpreted were misguided
information that became misunderstood

Sorrow is not a gift that we
should receive with gladness
We should resist the temptation
by focusing on Gods steadfastness

It is the joy that is within
that brushes or sorrows away
so that we can face life with peace
and joy each and every day

The Lord delights in those who fear Him,
who put their hope in His unfailing love.

Psalm 147:11

Conditions of Love

Humanly love comes
With many conditions

but

Heavenly love comes
through hours and day
of submission

Do You Really Love?

Love is not the mystery that
others have made it seem
Love is not just a feeling that flows
away with every summer breeze

Love is not an act that must
be performed from day to day
Love is a gift from God that is
unconditional in every way

For true love is not self-centered
neither envious or jealous too
Love is sacrificial and has no
limits to what it can do

Love is this wonderful gift
with rewards one cannot describe
but many do not receive this reward
because they operate with the love of a
Pharisee or a scribe

If you truly have the gift to love step
up and lead the way for many of
us are confused about it and have led
others astray

LOVE IS

Love is not a simple task
nor is it easily performed
It requires an unlimited amount
of unselfish acts that are not always
favorable among the norm

Love is often misconstrued
as an emotion that is limited by the way
we feel but love involves so much, much
more than one can actually reveal

Love is kind, love is gentle
And compassionate to one another
Love is not envious of other sisters of
brothers
Love is long suffering and will always bear
a lot
Love has no conditions to what
it will do or what it will not

Love is not jealous nor does it hold
malice in its heart
Love is a place where God abides
right from the very start

Love is not judgmental
nor does it look down upon others
Love knows that it must be patient
with the faults of another

LOVE

LOVE

can mean many things when
it is shared by those who truly care
In life there are times when situations
are good and times when situations look
bad but when love is true and pure
things that seem bad can work out to your
good

LOVE

can become a test sometimes
especially for those who are called by the
Most High
When in doubt or somewhat perplexed
there is only one sure thing that you can
do

TRUST

in God, King of all Kings
Leave it with Him because He
will stick closer than any friend
He will teach you both how to love His
way so that the love that's inside each of
you grows stronger and deeper each and
every day

Are You A Lover For Christ?

Self-Checklist

- Suffers long and is kind
- Does not envy
- Praises not one self
- Does not behave improperly
- Not easily provoked
- Hates sin, but loves righteousness
- Endures all things
- Believes all things
- Bears all things

Well, how did you do?

I face your temple as I worship, giving thanks to you for all your loving kindness and your faithfulness, for your promises are backed by all the honor of your name.

Psalm 138:2 TLB

Seeing What The Eye Cannot See

Many times we face challenges that
threaten to destroy our very existence
Do not fear them for these are only surface
appearances
What the eyes see is not what the Holy
Spirit knows
We must see our situations through the
Spirit instead of the flesh by giving God
complete control

The flesh wars against the Spirit trying to
keep us from seeing the truth
The truth that God is the only one who
will take care of you
No matter the challenge no matter the
problem
The only way to be victorious is to trust
God to solve them

Faith is the substance of things hoped for
and the evidence of things not seen
It would not be faith if we already had
what we supposedly dreamed

When the flesh plays with your thoughts
to make things seem worse that they really
are
Remember that view from the Spirit
is not the same by far

Life's Constant Roller Coaster Ride

Life is a constant roller coaster ride
Filled with curves and turns, lows and highs
For some don't mind the rides filled with thrills while others prefer to remain calm and still

Either way, life is going to offer us both the same
A ride filled with some joy, sorrow, laughter and some pain
We must learn to embrace ourselves for a ride with the unknown
'Cause it is there whether we embrace it or just moan and groan

There are paths in life we all have to face
Regardless of our profession, our status, our creed or our race
God never promised us a life with no storms but He did promise to guide us through it with no danger or harm

We are expected to mature and grow during those bumpy and uncomfortable times

'Cause there is wisdom to gain from every one of our tears and from every one of our whines

God promised to put no more on us than we can bear but while we are there, know that
He loves us and that He cares

Paying The Piper

Those tests you take are sometimes hard to face
They are constant afflictions that can cause pain and heartache
It is necessary for you to bear the burdens of the cross
For you are sheep to be slaughtered and must pay the cost

You can wiggle, you can whine, and you can even belly ache
but you will never escape those tiny little tests that you must take
Although it gets rough and often hard to bear
Remember those who have gone before you and have made it there

There is no task, no cross that you cannot beat
Your faith will determine your victory or you defeat
So brave those tests and face those heavy storms
With Christ on your side how can you go wrong

He will put no more on you than you can bear
He will give you the strength so that you can always prevail
He will comfort and hold you in those darkest hours
He will hide you from the shadow that seeks to devour

The love and faith that reigns deep in your heart
Is what will lead you to victory at the very start?

LIFE!

Life is filled with hopes, dreams and fantasies
Some remain just that and while some become reality
Real or not the mind will find a reason to escape
Especially when it is faced with overwhelming decisions, disappointment, sorrow or heartache.

Life's challenges are often difficult to bear at times
We often feel like giving or just throwing in the towel
Regardless of what path life throws our way
Remember the only solution to life's trials is to pray

On our knees vulnerable as the morning sun
We can openly make confessions to Jesus Christ, the Son
That no matter how strong we may appear to most
Our true source of strength derives from His Spirit, the Holy Ghost

We are often reminded that we are human beings weak and frail
And that without Him we are nothing and cannot prevail

Our cries of sorrow and pain that comes from time to time
Our Lord reminds us they last for just a short while

The overall message for us to know
is that our burdens are not ours alone
We bear them so that we can
encourage other lost souls

SEARCHING!

Searching for answers in all the wrong places
Trying to fill the void of those empty spaces

God is the answer for which we seek
Only through His love will we
find true and complete peace

It is not found in drugs or alcohol
It is not found in fornication
with another lost soul

It is not found in psychics and horoscopes
It is only through the
Spirit of the Holy Ghost

It is in God we must
Put all of our trust
and by His grace and mercy
He will deliver us

God is not willing that any should perish but that all should come to repentance.

11 Peter 3:9 KJV

With God It Is Never Too late

God our Creator is the true originator
to a precious gift called forgiveness
It is never too late to confess your faults
because of His grace, mercy and
tenderness

God is faithful God is true
To abide by the words that He has set
before you
He is unlike the world's natural man
Who changes his words and mind
whenever he can

His forgiveness will last till the end of time
His mercy for us last for many lifetimes
Once forgiven you are guaranteed a brand
new start
Beginning with a new heart

Don't think that you have done so much
that God does not hear you anymore
God is patient and id waiting for you
to open up your hearts door

Just open your heart and let Him in
Repent and ask Him to forgive you of your
sins
For this is the greatest gift He can ever give

A brand new life with a brand new beginning

SALVATION

Jesus is the truth the light and the way
So come and give your life today

You do not know what tomorrow will bring
Death or destruction to name a few of those things

Jesus is the key to your salvation
With one wave of his hand He can destroy any nation

As you surrender to His complete control
Jesus will bring peace and joy to your soul

With Me

Come
Walk with me for my yoke is easy

Come
Walk with me for my burdens are light

Come
Walk with me and I will give you strength

To
Walk with me into a new life

Rejoice

Away,
Away in a manger
There was born a
Savior for all
The world to see

Rejoice! Rejoice!
Oh, let us rejoice
For soon
He comes for thee

Path to Righteousness

The path of righteousness
Is narrow
And the way is
Very straight

It is the path that
Leads to God's kingdom
And through His pearly gates

So stay on the straight and narrow

THE SPIRIT

Be ye transformed by the renewing of your mind. Then you will be able to test and approve what God's will is his god, pleasing and perfect will.

Romans 12:2 AMP

Struggling To Be Free

Every day we are faced with trials and tribulations
That seem to dampen our weary souls
Yet we know God is there to help guide us
And keep us in complete control

It is such a struggle, a war constantly
Going on in our feeble little minds
Trying to take hold of the thoughts that
Toss and turn around and around
While pulling on every side

Struggling to be free from life's cocoon
Prisons of many persecutions
As we are challenged to rise above our everyday
Problems with rational spiritual solutions

Hoping one day to replace all our problems
With triumphs and victories so
That we may share them with others
In the life through our testimonies

God is the key controller to every thought
No matter what the kind
Our love, our faith, our trust in Him
Is the only way truly free our minds?

Keep in thought that the struggle
To be free is not quite ours alone
Our answer lies in God, our Creator
And our Savior who sits high
But looks down low

The Mind

The battlefield takes place in the mind
Forces pulling on every side
We are constantly going around and around
Trying to plant ourselves on solid ground

Sometimes we must let go of old things and friends
In order to build a new life in him
Things of old can lead us astray
And send us back to those wicked evil ways

The wrath of God can be very severe
To those who refuse to listen or hear
He will always make a way of escape
That sometimes we just refuse to take

Remember that our adversary never takes a vacation
He knows which way you go
So believe that he waits for you in the valley below

Thank God! For His mercy and kindness
Because through Him we can find forgiveness
My Lord will not always strive with you
Especially those who refuse to do

Be wise and stay away from all
That Satan will use others to say
He will cheat and lie until he is blue
He will use all that he can to turn you
From the truth, the light and the only way

My Lord Jesus Christ!

The Decay Of The Mind

A decaying mind is a mind temporarily without hope
One filled with despair and desperation to cope

A decaying mind is a mind without God's vision
Lost in a corrupt world with too many wrong decisions

A decaying mind is a mind that has been led astray
By the blind, the weak and those who lost their way

Yet, a decaying mind is not without hope
It is a mind that must be renewed
By the spirit of the Lord
The Holy Ghost

Meditating on the word of god night, noon, and day
Builds an inner strength in the mind against
The sins of the world today

Without this strength, the once decayed mind

Returns to be filled with thoughts
Once more that are corrupted by sinful thrills

The hold on this decaying mind this time
Is seven times greater than the first
You'll feel that your mind is confused
And that it is about to burst

Remember that once you decaying mind is clear
Be careful of what you hear, what you see
And extra careful of whom you are near

Battling Forces

The battlefield of this spiritual war begins
With the thoughts in our mind
There are forces pushing for control
Grabbing on every side

We must keep our mind refreshed
With the powerful words of the Lord
That is the only way to combat
Those evil and wicked thoughts

Once we begin to yield and
To lay our guards down
The enemy sneaks in and begins
To unstable our spiritual ground

Confusion, fear and doubt are rigor mortis
To our spiritual man within
It begins to spread in our lives until it has
endowed us with the foolishness of sin

We are constantly flipping and tossing
From one thought to another
Confusing the messages God gave us to
share with our lost sisters and brothers

The tool of the mind is a weapon of war
that is used to communicate.

Be careful of what you see and hear because a mind is a terrifying thing to waste.

For the enemy roams the earth seeking whom he may devour.
Knowing that time is limited and that we are in our final hour.

So search the scriptures every morning, noon, and night because it
Is in them you will regain your strength to Stand and to fight.

RENEW DAILY!

Renewing Of The Mind

The struggles of the flesh and the wars in
our mind can sometimes leave us blind
To the very things we hope to see
But we think will never be

GOD is the Creator of our mind, body and
soul because of his love, He leaves the
choice to serve Him in our control
Decisions, decisions, so many decisions
One could get lost without God's clear
vision

Our fate lies in the very steps that we take
As we struggle to love the very things that
we hate
It all comes down to this one bottom line:

"We can only succeed in God by the
renewing of our minds!"

Many, O Lord my God, are the wonderful works that you have done, and your thoughts toward us: none can compare with you! If I should declare and speak of them they are too many to be Numbered.
Psalm 40:5 AMP

A Humble Roar

Early one Sunday morning as I rose I felt the warmth from the rays
Of the sun. As my eyes stretched towards heaven, my spirit began to hum.

Behold the Lord in all his glory, as the sky glistened with the beauty of His grace.
A grace that is new to us each and every morning, which I have come to welcome and to embrace.

A warm sensation began to cover me like a glove fits over a hand.
I knew that God was present because my spirit man began to stand.

Lord, what would you ask of me and how can I be of service to you today?
He spoke very gently to my heart, "Would you please begin to pray."

I got on my knees and slowly stretched out my body face down to the floor.
A sudden sadness began to take a hold of me; a feeling I have never felt before.

Tears began to flow from my eyes and rolled softly onto the wooden floor.

My mouth cried out, "Abba Father", as tongues of fire made its humble roar.

God has been saddened by His people who live in the world today.
They have truly forgotten His commandments and let evil have its
Way.

Woe unto those who have the nerve to mislead others and cause
Them to go astray.
For tribulation you will see all of your life until your dying day.

Woe unto those who have used the gospel for profit or for selfish
Gain. For you will suffer with heartache and all kinds of sickness and pain.

To those who have been steadfast
And unmoved in their faith
Blessings and honor are your reward
As God continuously prepares your place

The lesson you see here should be quite clear but here it is just in case:

"Take heed to what you say to others
And consistently check the motives of your heart

There are severe consequences to those
Who play with the truth of the gospel and
to those who will worship false gods?"

A Life Without The Lord

A life without the Lord id no life at all!

Your life becomes empty with notions
That have no justifiable reason
This emptiness inside continues through season after season

Why you are here, for what purpose were you created?
To roam the earth with a heart filled with malice and filled with self-hatred

Your soul dampened with sadness waiting for the chance to cry out
Waiting to confess its sins
Waiting to give its shout

Peace, what is that? Joy, you do not know
Contentment is thy enemy and love is never shown
A man that says there is no God is often called a fool
For god is truly alive with an offer to live inside of you!

A Parable of Sowers

The Christians Guide to a Successful Crop

Those who sow by the wayside
Often fall because of the traditions of men
Manmade rules and devices that lead us
Nowhere but to heartache and sin

Those who sow on rocky ground
are superficial and are lacking in their faith
Their hope is not invested in the Lord
but in horoscopes and false saints

Those who have sown on thorny ground
are often mixed up in their priorities
They choke the life out of their own fruit
and always end up telling a sad story

Those who have sown on good ground
where the soil is rich to bear much fruit
are faithful and victorious sowers that
will always triumph and produce

Whatever you sow, you shall reap
so be careful of where you have
sown your seeds!

Appearances

Appearances are deceitful
and should not be considered

For it is the heart of the person
you should take heed of not the
surface of their demeanor!

For the Lord God is a sun and shield; the Lord bestows favor and honor; no good thing does He withhold from those whose walk is blameless. O Lord Almighty, Blessed is the man who trusts in you.

Psalm 84:11, 12 (TLB)

Prosperity

Look to the Lord

in all that you do

Then you will find that

He will allow you to

prosper too

And in your prosperity,

You will not be moved!

Yielding

If I should let you
come through me Lord
strong and bold!
Oh! The mysteries that
You would unfold

As I look out toward the sky,
I see heaven opening
before my eyes

Doves and eagles
flying everywhere
This feeling within
I cannot compare

Peace reigning deep
In my heart
So much within, I do not
know where to start

Overwhelmed by what I see
JESUS reaching out his hand
to me!

O Lord!

O Lord,

help me to give Thee praise everyday
so that no matter where I am or what I am
doing the steps I take will not be in vain

O Lord,

help me to remember to show
the same love and mercy that You have
shown me to another sister or brother

O Lord,

help me to pray throughout the night and day
Not so much for myself but for those who have lost their way

Finally,
give me strength, O Lord, to run this race

Cling

Cling to me Oh Jesus

Cling to my side of the cross

Cling to me Oh Jesus
so that my soul never gets lost

Cling, cling, and cling much more
 'cause today I face temptations
I have never seen before

CLING!

The Answer Lies Within

Within our heart the truth we know always abided
It is sometimes hidden by temptations that are often disguised

Worry is a disguise that hides the confidence we have in Christ
It takes away our peace and replaces it with strife

Being anxious is another that steals the truth from us too
By getting us to solve our own problems instead of waiting to see what God will do

Confusion is by far the worst of any of those lies
Its' tricky and deceptive moves leave us double-minded in our minds on every side

So, what is the key that reveals our hidden truth?
Well, it is not through the psychic networks or horoscopes too

It is through prayer that we unlock the door to the answers that lie within

Prayer has the power to rid us from worry, anxiety, confusion and even sin

God Is Standing Near

No matter what situation
you are facing right now
No matter how it may appear
Know that you are not alone
but that God is standing near

He understands your inner most thoughts
and how you hurt from all this pain
With His love He hides you under his wing
to shelter you from the rain

There is no problem He cannot fix
no pain He cannot heal
There is no unknown enemy
that his love will not reveal

Hold on just for a little while longer
your help is on its way
For soon you will find your problem gone
and once again peace will regin

Never return evil for evil or evil insult for insult… But on the contrary blessing—praying for their welfare, happiness and protection and truly pitying them and loving them. For know to this you have been called, blessing (from God) obtain a blessing as heirs, bring welfare and happiness and protection

1 Peter 3:9 AMP

Unconditional Love

Don't pass judgment

on one another

Stop and Pick up

that sister or brother

For this is the way of our Lord

A love that is unconditional to all!

Children Don't Love The Same

Children don't love the same way as you and I
Their love is special and one of a kind
It is a love that is trusting of everyone young or old
Their love has no limits, no conditions and no mysteries to unfold

The love that they show is both innocent and pure
They love you no matter what you say or no matter what you do
Children have a love that we should all hope one day to gain
A love that treats their enemies and their friends just the same

Their love is faithful to forgive without charging a price
A love given with no cost for its many sacrifice
Children are mankind's guides to that heavenly place
That is free from reproach, reprisal and simple mistakes

Children are precious gifts from God filled with His love at birth
A love given to them to share with us while we are here on earth

Children learn to hold grudges from the adults who have forgotten
That love is unconditional to all, good or rotten

So stop, look and listen to all that children do and say
Because children hold the answers to many problems that arise today

A Mother's Love

A mother is a vessel of honor
filled with love from the Lord above
With their love they surround us
like the open wings of a gentle dove

No matter how often we stumble
No matter how often we fall
A mother's love is guaranteed
to be with us through it all

A mother's love is precious
like rubies, diamonds and pearls
It is a rare and unique gift
not often found in this whole world

Her love is unconditional
to sons and daughters the same
This is why we honor her
although she never claims her fame

So, if you are lucky to have a mom
who is as special as mine
Treasure her and keep her dear
for she is worth more than all
the silver, platinum and gold combined

A Father's Love

To be a father is truly an honor
a blessing given by God
It comes with an enormous responsibility
that is sometimes challenging and
sometimes hard

Remember that you are the head,
Not the tail
Or anything that falls in between
Born into this world a great prince
You were crowned a king
By the King of all Kings

The love that flows is not the same
As the love given by our dear mothers
It is a love that is strong and warm
Given equally to every son and daughter

You are the strength of your family
And the backbone to our every thought
We honor you on Father's Day
Because of the battles that you have fought

We appreciate your wisdom, your caring
And the gentleness that the world doesn't
often see
The way that you guide us with discipline
To bring our lives to complete victory

It is a blessing, an honor to call you my Dad
For life without you would have been lonesome and sad

So, know that you are appreciated in every way
For the love and guidance you have shown each and every day

A Marriage From Heaven

A marriage made in heaven
Is made from God above
It is a marriage that is centered
on God's true love

There may be some problems
that are common from time to time
but when God is at the helm
everything will work out fine

The key to the success of this
marriage made from heaven
Is that God is the one who put it together
from the very beginning

But God demonstrates his own love for us in this: while we were still sinners, Christ died for us. Since we have now been justified by his blood, how much more shall we be saved from God's wrath through him!

Romans 5:8-9 (AMP)

The Price

During the times

Of Jesus Christ

Christ gave his

life to pay a price

For the remission

of our sins

So that we may

begin a new life

in Him!

Judgment

Judgment Day is very near
It is time for all the world to hear
That the end of this world is coming soon
so don't get caught unsaved of you are doomed

The gospel is being spread throughout the nation
It is time to give up the world system and come into salvation
For this is not a game you see
Only Jesus Christ can set you free

Free from all the tricks of Satan
Who has men blinded across the nation
It is time to get our lives in check
Through Jesus Christ there is hope for you yet!

Don't shake this off and throw this away
It is through this message you could be saved

Get on your knees and repent of your sins
Believe and confess that He's your friend
Praise and ask Him to come in and He will give you a new life in him

A Recipe For Salvation

You will need the Following ingredients:

A Heart
A cup of repentance
An ounce of love
A tablespoon of the Holy Spirit
Fellow Christians
A Church
The Master

Directions:

1. Pour into the heart a cup of repentance.
2. Add an ounce of love and stir.
3. Then add a tablespoon of the Holy Spirit and shake until a change comes.
4. Mix with your fellow Christians.
5. Pour into a church
6. Test to see if all is done
7. Now serve the Master

Standing In Line

We have become a people committed to
standing in lines for items that are often
free
Free food, free tickets, free money
and even a free shopping spree

We will even stand in a line
for a three to four night vacation
but we will not stand in God's line
for the free gift of salvation

Now here's a free gift that is
guaranteed to save your very life
Instead, we by-pass this short line
To satisfy another appetite
Why?

Sin is fun and has become
quite enjoyable to you
so enjoyable that you have gotten
comfortable acting like a fool

Comfortable or not, sin comes
with an enormous price to pay
A life where the soul is lost and eternally
damned with no chance for hope again

The next time that you decide to stand

in one of those very long, long lines
First, make sure that you have stood in line
for your soul to be saved by
God Almighty, the Most High

A Nation Renewed

We are a nation saddened by
the corrupt choices we have made
Choices that led us to turn our back on God
And let righteousness slip away

We must repent and ask God for
forgiveness of our foolish and sinful ways
So that His peace, mercy and grace
can once again reign

Otherwise, we are doomed as
many nations have been in the past
Nations who thought that God would
allow their sins to go unmasked

The covers are off and sin has now been revealed
As a nation crippled by corruption,
waiting to be healed

Our nation's healing is just a simple touch away
It begins as a nation when we collectively begin to pray
As we cry, "Lord please forgive us, we renounce our sins once more."

God then opens up the windows of heaven
and from his Spirit He begins to pour
Blessings, peace, mercy and love are just to
name a few
Of the wonderful gifts God has in store
for a nation that has been renewed!

Declaring God's Glory

A FATHER'S LOVE

By
Monique R. Ransom
Prophetess

About the Author

Inspiring Author and Motivational Speaker Monique is a native of the great city of New York. Monique R. Ransom is the mother of four bright wonderful beautiful children and an employee in the Baltimore City Public School as an IEP Chair.

She graciously draws from the Lord's spirit, poetry filled with astounding words that will encourage, uplift, chasten, and provide hope for the soul.

Educated in the New York Public School System, she graduated with a Business Degree from Adelphi University. It wasn't until her first child was born that she became inspired to seek a career in education. She adds to her accomplishments a Master's in Education from Coppin State University. She is currently pursuing her Doctorate in Divinity.

She was given this vision from God ten years ago. It is her calling to minister from her heart and soul to those who have gone astray; to those who are broken hearted, and those who are imprisoned in their minds.

Each word, each verse is an expression of wisdom from her own trials and tribulations. The prayers and anecdotes that she uses to combat her own challenges and the hardship that she faces daily in her life, she now shares them with us.

So, journey with her as she opens the gates of hell to set the captives free.

Our Mission is Clear!

The Spirit of the Lord God is upon me for he hath anointed me to preach good tidings to the meek. He hath sent me to bind up the broken hearted, to proclaim liberty to the captives, and the opening of the prison to them that are bound.

To proclaim the acceptable year of the Lord and the day of vengeance of our God; to comfort all that mourns; to appoint unto them that mourn in Zion; to give unto them beauty for ashes, oil of joy for mourning, the garment of praise for the spirit of heaviness; that they might be called trees of righteousness, the planting of the Lord, that He might be glorified!

Isaiah 61:1-4

Through His Grace and Mercy
Thou Can Be Saved!

The Bible says, "That if Thou shalt confess with thy mouth the Lord Jesus and shall believe in thine heart that God raised Him for the dead, Thou shalt be saved. For with the heart man believeth unto righteousness; and with the mouth confession is made unto salvation."
(Romans 10:9, 10)

If you would receive Jesus Christ as Lord and Savior of your life, with sincerity, pray from your heart:

Lord Jesus,

I believe that You died for me and that You rose again on the third day. I confess to You that I am a sinner and that I need Your love and forgiveness. Come into my life, forgive my sins, give my life its meaning and make me whole again. Give me eternal life. I confess You now as my Lord and Savior. Thank you for my salvation!

If you made this confession, we would like to hear from you.

Who Is Thy Neighbor?

This profound book takes a real hard look at the heart of Christian soul and the role the church should take in respect to being a good neighbor and a Good Samaritan.

This book is centered on the parable of the Good Samaritan and depicts the life of a fictional character named Jasmine to illustrate how to be a good neighbor to one another. Read about Jasmine's seasons of change. See how God moves her from isolation to revelation. Test your own heart and see where it lays.

This is a 206 page power packed book of knowledge you won't want to pass up which includes in the book a study guide for group activity.

Purchase at http://www.moniqueransomministries.com

Can A Christian Be Possessed By An Evil Spirit?

I know what you are thinking, but don't let the title fool you. This profound book looks beyond the question into a deeper concern of how throughout the years we have twisted the meaning of God's Words leaving us with misconceptions and unsubstantiated truths. God tells us in Hosea 4:6 that "My people suffer for lack of knowledge" and believe me, we have.

This book revolutionizes the way we have perceived much of God's Word and set us a new path of enlightenment of Biblical truths.

Purchase at
http://www.moniqueransomministries.com

Our Pathway For Communication
is
Now Open!

Reaching out to others is important to us.
We would love to hear from you.
To contact us:

Visit Our Websites:

http://www.firsttouch.us

or

http://www.moniqueransomministries.com

By Email:

shespeaks3@aol.com

Facebook

http://www.facebook.com/biblethumperlily

www.ingramcontent.com/pod-product-compliance
Lightning Source LLC
Chambersburg PA
CBHW071122090426
42736CB00012B/1980